GREAT YARMOUTH TRAMWAYS

Series editor Robert J Harley

David Mackley

Cover picture: All of the Great Yarmouth electric trams were built to a similar format and to 'off the peg' designs of the Brush Electric Engineering Co. of Loughbrough. Car 9, seen here at Wellington Pier, is one of the original 1902 batch which were rebuilt in the 1920s. Of these, 9 was one of the few to be re-equipped with the type AA truck which was standard for all later batches of cars. (A. D. Packer)

Published July 2003

ISBN 1 904474 13 6

Design   Deborah Esher
*   David Pede*
Typesetting   Barbara Mitchell

Published by
*   Middleton Press*
*   Easebourne Lane*
*   Midhurst, West Sussex*
*   GU29 9AZ*
Tel: 01730 813169
Fax: 01730 812601
Email: enquiries@middletonpress.fsnet.co.uk

Printed & bound by Biddles Ltd, Kings Lynn

CONTENTS

INTRODUCTION & ACKNOWLEDGEMENTS

This volume would not have been possible without the researches and generosity of others. Roy Anderson's *Tramways of East Anglia* remains a standard work while the late Terry Barker's *Transport in Great Yarmouth* is unrivalled for detail. Technical and historical material, some of it unpublished hitherto, comes from the Public Record Office, Norfolk County Record Office and Birmingham City Library.

Following the loss of the official photograph album, the Great Yarmouth Transport Department compiled a replacement collection from other sources and I am grateful to First Bus, the successor organisation, and Norfolk Record Office for allowing use of images filed under reference BR 272/135. The remaining pictures come from eighteen organisations and individuals who have both been generous and helpful. Inivitably, some images have turned up in more than one collection. Every effort has been made to accurately attribute them.

Historical and anecdotal material was provided by P. Allard, A.W. Bond, P. Carver, L. Cockrill, G. Kenworthy, T. Major, M. Metcalf, L. Seabert, L.J. and Y.D. Steward and E. Wisker. The Bodleian Library provided some maps. Those used are from the Ordnance Surveys of 1905/6 and 1927/8 as indicated.

Peter Larter gave many hours preparing images while, local historian Colin Tooke kindly checked the text for accuracy after my wife, Kathrine, had typed a legible version. Godfrey Croughton kindly supplied the tickets.

Gaps remain in the record concerning the first horse tram depot in Southtown Road. Photographs of depot interiors have eluded the author, as have tramway scenes south of St Peters Road, of North Quay, of Fullers Hill and of the long straight from Newtown to Caister. The author would like to hear from any reader able to fill these gaps.

This volume is dedicated to two generations of tramway staff, human and equine, who provided a service, often in conditions that would not be countenanced today. To those who recorded their deeds, in words and pictures, we are much indebted.

GEOGRAPHICAL SETTING

Great Yarmouth is the most easterly town in Norfolk and the county's second largest settlement. It is situated on a shingle spit, first developed as an island across the mouth of a large estuary which once stretched as far as Norwich, just over 20 miles to the west. Today, the rivers Bure and Waveney form a confluence with the River Yare at Breydon Water, a large tract of tidal water to the west of Yarmouth. From here, the River Yare flows broadly parallel to the sea-shore before discharging into the North Sea at the harbour mouth.

Gorleston stands mostly on higher ground and on the western bank of the Yare's lower reaches.

It partly faces the South Denes of Great Yarmouth and partly the open sea. Its beaches form a shallow bay to the south of the harbour mouth.

The coastal village of Caister-on-Sea lies two and a half miles to the north of Great Yarmouth. It partly occupies rising ground which had been on the northern shore of the ancient estuary.

The largely level terrain of Great Yarmouth and gentle gradients of Gorleston presented few challenges to tramway engineers. However, for economic and political reasons, they were never to apply their skills to a river crossing at Yarmouth Haven.

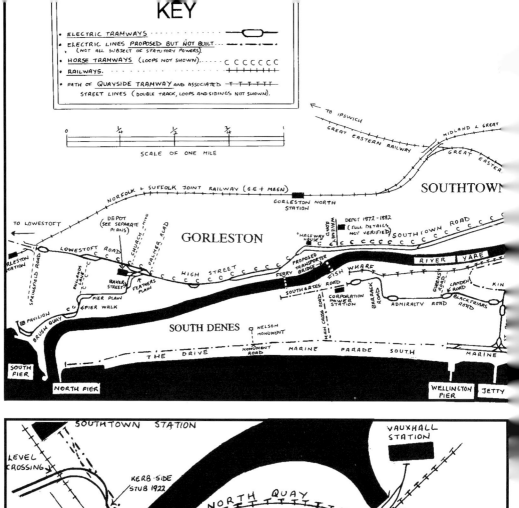

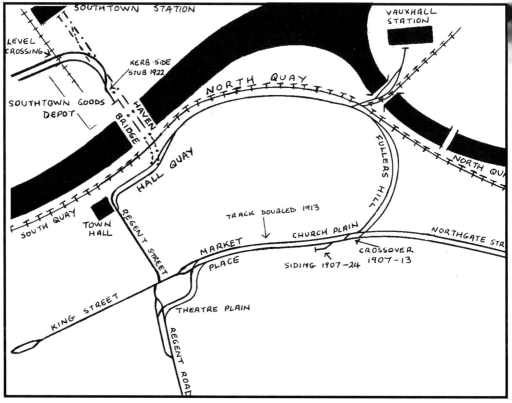

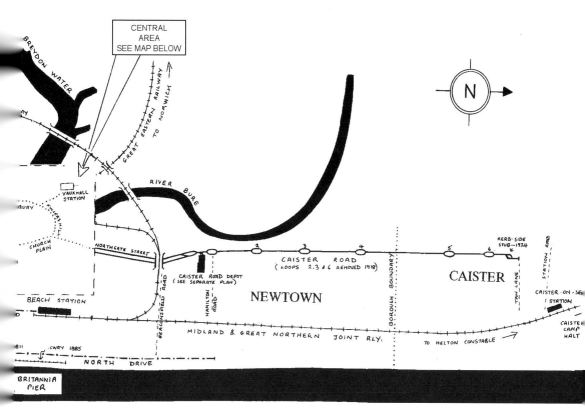

HISTORICAL BACKGROUND

Great Yarmouth owes its economic existence to herring. In 1000 AD its site was being used as a base for fishermen following the migratory shoals. In 1209, King John granted a charter to what had become a flourishing town. Town walls were completed in the 14th century, substantial lengths of which remains, as do other antiquities including the fine St Nicholas' Church, reputedly the largest parish church in England.

Great Yarmouth has three faces. The river has been the focus of the herring fishery, curing, canning, ship-building and maritime trade. Today, North Sea oil and gas industries have partly filled the gap left by a declined fishery. The Market Place, described as the largest and finest in England is still flourishing today, though only with local trade. The modern holiday resort is mostly situated on The Denes, poor and previously largely undeveloped land between the town walls and the sea. A growing watering place, it was fashionable with the 'well to do' by the end of the eighteenth century. In the nineteenth the railway brought 'the masses', notably from the midlands and the north. Until 1959, the town had three railway termini; two of them linked to a

quayside tramway which predated the tramways depicted in this book by more than thirty years and outlived them by more than forty.

Great Yarmouth is a linear town with many of its main thoroughfares running north to south. Within the old town, 145 densely populated and narrow alleyways known as 'rows', ran from east to west, thereby creating a grid street pattern. These have largely succumbed to wartime bombing and redevelopment, but some fascinating traces remain.

The first bridge across Yarmouth Haven to what is now Southtown was built in 1427. From then on, the interdependence of Yarmouth, Southtown and Gorleston developed, and all are now part of the Borough of Great Yarmouth. For centuries all of Gorleston and much of Southtown had been part of Suffolk.

In the later Victorian period, Gorleston grew from a tiny fishing port to a small resort with a gentler character than its larger neighbour. This development along higher ground and cliff tops continued in the Edwardian years.

Caister was an important location for the Romans who built a shore fort there. For centuries,

Caister was primarily a fishing village until the railway and tramway brought visitors and commuters to develop the local economy. Caister became famous early in the last century as a result of the brave and, one time tragic, exploits if its lifeboatmen. "Caistermen never turn back" remains a village dictum.

The East Anglian Tramway Order of 1871 paved the way for a continuous tramway from Southtown to Southwold via Gorleston and Lowestoft, a total distance of 20 miles. Only two quite separate lengths were actually built. In 1903, Lowestoft Corporation opened an electrified line, mostly within their Borough boundaries. The other was the line from Southtown Station to Feathers Plain at Gorleston which was opened in 1875 by the East Anglian Tramways Company. This was the first street tramway in East Anglia. Those at Ipswich and Cambridge followed five years later. The line was laid to standard gauge on longitudinal wooden sleepers. Only one passing loop was provided. The service was half-hourly. Cars and horses operated from a depot by Southtown Road.

The tramway's birth had been protracted, work having started in 1872. It was sold in 1876 and again in 1878, latterly to the Yarmouth and Gorleston Tramways Company.

By 1882, that company had replaced the original deficient track with girder rails gauged to 3ft 6ins, installed more loops and opened a new depot in Feathers Plain. A new terminal was put in immediately to the west of Southtown Bridge. In Gorleston, the new line terminated near 'The Ship' inn in Englands Lane via an extension along Lowestoft Road. This line was later extended to a summer terminus on Brush Quay.

By the end of the century, the company was struggling financially. The British Electric Traction Company took control in 1900, with the aim of electrifying the line as part of a larger scheme to operate electric trams throughout the Borough.

However, these plans were elbowed aside when the Borough Council disclosed its own intention to operate electric trams; initially in Great Yarmouth itself. The 3ft 6ins (1067 mm) gauge system was opened on 19th June 1902. A depot for 14 trams was built adjacent to the Newtown terminus. Traction current was provided from the Corporation's own generating station. Total route mileage was 3.72 miles / 6km laid with 90lb per yard Belgian rail. Two basic services were provided and with route permutations, one from Vauxhal Station and one from Newtown, both terminating at Wellington Pier. Unfortunately the system plan was drawn up with some haste to obtain statutory approval. Consequently, lines in St Peters Road and Fullers Hill were never profitable and the failure to install double track for the length of Regent Road at the outset was a continual cause of congestion and delay.

In 1904, the Borough purchased the Gorleston line and, for a short time, became the operator of horse trams and also horse buses. The track in England's Lane was lifted and a new line to Gorleston Beach (by the Pavilion) put in via Baker Street, Pier Plain and Brush Quay. The Lowestoft Road line was extended to just north of the bridge at the not long opened Gorleston railway station. The new electrified service was ceremonially opened on 4th July 1905 and was virtually self contained, all but heavy repairs to cars being undertaken at a new depot at Feather Plain. At Gorleston, cars terminated at the Beach or Station alternately.

In Yarmouth, the final stage of a new line to the Fish Wharf was opened in 1905. This also served the racecourse which was situated on the South Denes at the time.

1907 saw the last extension; from Newtown and across the Borough boundary to Caister. This line was a long straight across open countryside and was punctuated by passing loops. It brought the total mileage of the combined tramways to 9.94 / 16km miles. Further extensions were considered but not constructed in the years before World War I, but track in the Market Place was doubled in 1913.

The Borough's plans included a line across Haven Bridge to connect the two parts of the system but a new bridge was required. Negotiations with the Port and Haven Commisioners were entered into more than once but without agreement regarding the apportionment of cost. This put the tramways at a continuing disadvantage. Alternative schemes for a river crossing, including a tunnel and a trans porter bridge, were considered but not pursued.

World War I saw services much reduced and a manpower shortage, partly alleviated by recruitment of women conductors. By the end of hostilities, track and rolling stock were in a very run down condition.

Three secondhand London General 'B' type double deck buses were purchased in 1920 and provided a service from Southtown Station and across the Haven Bridge to the town centre and sea-front. Later they provided a service from the Town Hall to South Quay (Fishwharf) and covered the Caister service while the tram track was being repaired.

In 1923, the Corporation decided to renew the tramways by rebuilding the car fleet, laying new track and installing a signalling system. There was some rationalisation. The St Peters Road tracks were lifted and the Fishwharf service was converted to bus operation in 1924. Trams thus released were used to increase frequencies on other routes.

By 1927, however, the case in favour of the trams was weakening. Relaxation of permissible axle loadings improved the economics of bus operation and an agreement was reached on the construction of a new bascule bridge, but without provision of tram track. The gradual running down of the tramways became policy. The Vauxhall Station service ceased in 1929. In 1930, came the closure of the Gorleston to Southtown line; the most profitable of the system. The best Gorleston cars were transferred to the Yarmouth section which continued to operate until 1933, the last year in which the town's transport livery was to be maroon and cream. 1934 was to herald in the Blue Bus era.

On 14th December the last tram set off from the Market Place with the Mayor, Mr Peter Ellis, driving and Alderman Beevor; himself an old tramway man, acting as conductor to a heavy load of passengers, including local dignitaries and invited guests. The Chairman of the Transport Committee; Mr Barr, waxed sentimental with:

> *"Farewell old tram,*
> *no more can you be mended,*
> *Go rest in peace*
> *Your useful life has ended"*

The bodies of 23 of the 35 cars went to 'rest' as holiday camp chalets at Caister.

In 2000, Great Yarmouth Borough Council explored the possiblities of the Parry People Mover, as a format for a light tramway in Regent Road and on the sea front. This proposal remains 'on the table' at the time of writing. Meanwhile, the need for a rail link to a new outer harbour raises the possibility of a revived quayside tramway and the prospect of rails in the streets once more.

NEWTOWN TO WELLINGTON PIER

1.   Caister Road depot, adjacent to the then Newtown Terminus, is seen on 19th June 1902, the opening day of the electric tramway. A meeting of dignitaries and others is taking place while flags flutter from part of the overhead. Onlookers seem wary about intruding on the privacy of proceedings which were to become more public when three cars decorated with flags toured the system. The office building was later enlarged with an upper storey. The car sheds and workshops were extended in 1907. The scheme included three Edgar Allen turntables giving access to the repair and maintenance bays. (Colin Tooke coll.)

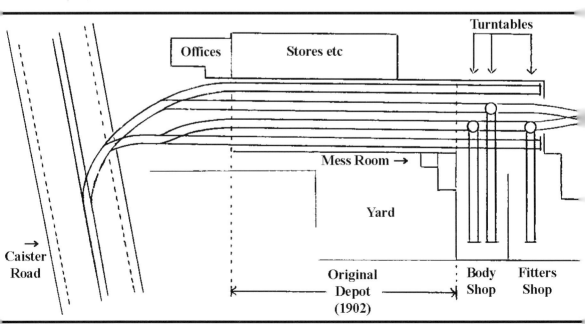

1907 depot plan.

2.　　In 1904, this distinctive passenger shelter was erected at the corner of Caister Road and Beaconsfield Road at a cost of £25. It remained in use for bus passengers until demolished in 1972. A similar shelter was provided at the Gorleston Station terminus in 1908. The structure survives but somewhat altered and incorporated into a Chinese takeaway. (Colin Tooke coll.)

3.　　Car 6 is seen here navigating flood waters, possibly in 1905 or 1912. The location is Northgate Street, between the corners of Stanley Road and Ormond Road. The tram is heading broadly south, but the driver is equipped to go south west. (Norfolk Heritage Centre)

4.   This scene probably dates from the late 1920s and records more flooding at the very same location as in the previous picture, but viewed from the opposite side of the road. Once again, car 6 cuts a watery path in company with another but unidentified car. (Colin Tooke coll.)

5.   Car 4's trolley arm is well swung out on its offset mast in this animated scene of Northgate Street in the mid 1920s. The workmen with the tower wagon are attending to a street light suspended from the tramway bracket arm. The frame of an earlier lamp sits empty on the top of the traction pole. The bus is an AEC YC of United Automobile Services. The chassis is a much rebuilt military vehicle fitted with a bus body at the operator's Lowestoft coach works. The bus has just passed the corner of Rampart Road while the tram is level with Frederick Road. (Peter Larter coll.)

6. A 1902 car traverses Church Plain on its way to the Market Place, about 1905. The range of attractive and historical buildings in the background remain to this day, including the one time home of the Victorian authoress, Anna Sewell, auther of "Black Beauty". The spire and much of the ancient interior of the fine St Nicholas parish church were destroyed by incendiary bombs in 1942. (Richard Adderson coll.)

7.   Car 10 here threads its way along the west side of the Market Place about 1905. Other traffic includes a Great Eastern Railway delivery van and a young lad with a wheelbarrow load of produce. Recent remodelling of the Market Place has thinned out the crowded stalls, but the combination of North Sea winter air and hot potato chips is still an experience to savour here.
(East Anglia Transport Museum coll.)

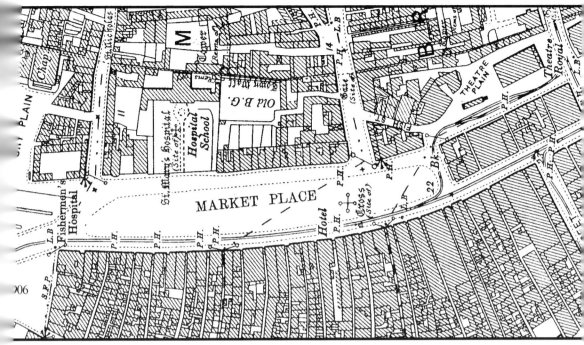

8.　　The track in the Market Place was doubled in 1913. It is seen here shortly after the major track renewal programme of 1926. A signalling system was installed at the same time. One of the lamp boxes can just be seen about four feet from the top of the traction column (centre right). This controlled the alternating bends into Theatre Plain. Lights for the control of general road traffic did not appear in Great Yarmouth until 1931. (Basil Gowen coll.)

9.	Car 6 is seen here shortly after World War I, before the fleet rebuilding programme in which anticlockwise staircases were fitted. Today, this side of the Market Place is a pedestrian zone. Most of the characterful buildings seen here on the east side have long since gone.
(National Tramway Museum)

10.	Car 31 waits in the Market Place by Palmers store on a rather wet day in 1932. At this point, part of the overhead was suspended from wall fixtures called 'rosettes', one of which can be seen between the two first floor bay windows. Another at the further end of the store was still in situ in 2003.
(Dr. Hugh Nicol/ National Tramway Museum)

11.　　Car 9 waits at the Market Place corner stop in 1932. The enamel stop sign on the traction pole is blue and white. This picture illustrates how the salt air of 'The Briny' (North Sea) could dull the paintwork of the Great Yarmouth cars. (M.J.O'Connor/National Tramway Museum)

12.　　At the corner of the Market Place, we see work progressing with the original trackwork of 1902. Palmers Store, seen to the left, was then already well established. It still trades today but behind a re-modelled frontage. (Colin Tooke coll.)

13. The Fish Wharf route was opened in stages, over two years. Car 4's stencil route indicator display reads "Queens Road", the early 1905 temporary terminus. The dark attire of some of the ladies serves as a reminder of one of Yarmouth's lesser known former industries, that of silk manufacture. Victorian 'mourning crepe' was a particular speciality. (Basil Gowen coll.)

→

14. A tram and three horse drawn vehicles including two buses, have just jostled for road space at the western end of Regent Road, looking towards King Street, in August 1902. The tram is confined to its rails, whereas the relative freedom of each bus requires three pairs of horses each day. "A Message from Mars" was the title of a presentation at the Theatre Royal, here obscured by the greenery to the right. Its site is now covered by part of the Market Gates shopping complex. (Colin Tooke coll.)

→

15. Facing in the opposite (easterly) direction the sweep of the rails from Theatre Plain into Regent Road and the line of the overhead are well portrayed in this scene from about 1930, as is the seemingly illogical reduction to single track beyond Alexandra Road. The gentleman by the tram stop to the left is, presumably, reading the label on a jar of shoe whitener. (Basil Gowen coll.)

16.   Car 9 has come to rest at the awkwardly sited stop at the sea front end of Regent Road in 1932. To the left is one of the ungainly Guy FCX three axle double deck buses delivered in 1928. The destination blind, sited in the rear dome, has already been set for the return trip from Wellington Pier to Gorleston Beach, by a path over Haven Bridge that no tram could follow.
(M.J. O'Connor/ National Tramway Museum)

17.   Also in 1932, car 32 of the 1907 batch is seen setting down passengers. To the right is one of five AEC Regent petrol buses acquired by the Corporation in 1931. These were the last buses to be painted in the tramway colours when new and before a predominantly blue livery was adopted in 1934.
(M.J. O'Connor/ National Tramway Museum)

18.   A 1902 car turns from Regent Road into Marine Parade, in October 1907. At this time, small destination boards were fixed above the upper deck side panels, having earlier been sited on the window ledges. A church congress is in session in the Royal Aquarium in the background, by now a theatre and public hall, though retaining its piscatorial title. To the right is the revolving tower, a 120 feet/36.5m high open framed steel structure. It was dismantled in 1941. (Basil Gowen coll.)

Aquarium, Revolving Tower, & Gardens, Gt. Yarmouth.

19.   At this point, we alight from our tram tour to visit the site of Great Yarmouth's first experience of electric traction. This was the railway of Henry Bock Binko which ran in 1885 from Britannia Pier for 400 yards northwards along the edge of the Denes. The track gauge was 'about 20 inches' and the train was powered by the "Ohm" electric locomotive marshalled in the middle of the train. Power came from a steam driven dynamo in the nearby Royal Aquarium. Electrical supply and return was through the running rails which were insulated as were the wheels, all of which picked up current. The Corporation would not agree to a longer line between Britannia and Wellington Piers. The shorter one, therefore, served solely as a demonstration and offered only a brief trip from 'somewhere' to 'nowhere' and back! Income fell far short of expenses. It transpired that Binko was already an undischarged bankrupt. The line was closed and taken up in August 1885; just six weeks after being laid. Binko could claim a place in history for at least two achievements. In 1884, his railway claimed to be the first to electrically transport British royalty. The elegant carriage in the photograph was built especially for the use of the Prince and Princess of Wales. Also, a version of his railway laid in Edinburgh had been the first electric street railway to operate from a fixed power source.
(Colin Tooke coll.)

20.   Resuming our tour, we find the expanse of the sea front portrayed in this southward view from the corner of Regent Road. The curved track appears to have been watered to ease the tram's passage towards Newtown. The date is 1929 or later as the single deck bus to the left is one of five Guy FBBs dating from that year. It is probably running on the Vauxhall Station to Wellington Pier service. An older Guy single decker and another tram can be seen further down the 'prom'.
(National Tramway Museum coll.)

21.   Seen here from a southbound tram in 1902, car 2 is heading north on Marine Parade between the turnings for Marlborough Terrace and Britannia Road. The virginia creeper on the promenade buildings has long since gone as has the symmetry of the terrace following the piece-meal conversion to small hotels and restaurants. Anecdotal evidence suggests that in 1902 the pedestrians could hail a tram to stop at any point on the system, the Corporation being anxious not to miss a fare! Designated stops were phased in between 1904 and 1912. (Colin Tooke coll.)

22.   A rebuilt 1902 car passes a 'bullnose' Morris late in the 1920s and amongst typical sea front holiday crowds of the period. The Britannia Pier Pavilion, seen here, was built in July 1914 to replace that burned down in April of the same year. An earlier conflagration had engulfed the structure in 1909. The tilted area on the pavement is on the site of the present day Leisureland amusements. The revolving tower platform is fully lowered. (Colin Tooke coll.)

23.   In this pre 1905 view from a little further south, three 1902 cars dominate the Parade traffic. The horse buses would disappear ere long, together with the beach yawls and bathing machines. In the background, the revolving tower platform is half up (or down). The Britannia Pier Pavilion is that destroyed by fire in 1909. The open air auditorium is the Singers Ring, home of Chappel's Promenade concert at the time. Not all is changed, however. Landaus, like that passing the nearest tram, are still a special feature of modern day Great Yarmouth. (Richard Adderson coll.)

24.   Car 13 is passing the St Peters Road corner on its way to Wellington Pier in 1902. Hanging from the traction pole is the pull wire to set the overhead 'frog' for cars turning to our left. The centre poles outlived the trams by several decades, the bracket arms being used to mount illuminations and coronation decorations. (Basil Gowen coll.)

25.   The photographer has climbed the old lookout tower by the Jetty to capture the installation of the elaborate and very expensive junction layout connecting St Peters Road and Marine Parade. Services along St Peters Road were never really viable and the track was removed during the 1923 upgrading of the remainder of the system. The Barking Smack Inn remains relatively unchanged today while the Bath Hotel, here seen surrounded by scaffolding, has since annexed the corner pub. Flamingo Amusements now occupy the ground floor. (Colin Tooke coll.)

26.   Marine Parade was still termed as The Drive when this heavily tinted postcard was produced about 1905. The publisher has gone to extraordinary lengths to portray the overhead wiring for the St Peters Road Junction. In Edwardian times, trams and their attendant street furniture were considered to be indicative of civic enterprise and modernity. (Basil Gowen coll.)

27.   Former Gorleston car 24 is seen here at the Wellington Pier terminus, in the 1930s. The tower wagon for overhead repairs seems to be a more elaborate affair than that seen in picture 52 and has seats over the rear tool lockers. At this time, a horse was hired from a local haulier as and when required. (A.D. Packer)

28.   A 1902 car approaches Wellington Pier terminus while a 1905 car (probably brand new and carrying no advertisements) departs. In the background are Albert Square and Kimberley Terrace. This is the more genteel end of the sea front and it remains relatively so; the mid nineteenth century buildings retain most of their dignity to this day. (Colin Tooke coll.)

29.   Two 1902 cars at the terminus show two arrangements of side route boards fixed to the window ledges. The operators title has not yet been applied to the rocker panels. This probably dates the picture as 1904, the magnificent Winter Gardens building having been opened in June of that year. It was bought second hand from Torquay. Its incandescent appearance, in this post card view, can probably be attributed to brand new glass and lots of fresh paint. (Basil Gowen coll.)

243/3   WINTER GARDENS, GT. YARMOUTH.

30.　　A quarter century after the date of the previous picture, rebuilt 1902 car 7 is having its upper deck seats turned to face the direction of Newtown. No doubt this car and others would later be conveying patrons to the Evening Follies advertised in the tram window. This entertainment was on offer for the 1929 to 1931 summer seasons. (A.D.Packer)

31.　　The upper deck panel of this car declares "Gorleston-on-Sea, the place for health, pleasure and beauty. Cars from Southtown Bridge every few minutes. Return fare 4d". The distinctive Wellington Pier pavilion of 1903 and neighbouring Winter Gardens remain as the prominent features of the present day sea front. (National Tramway Museum coll.)

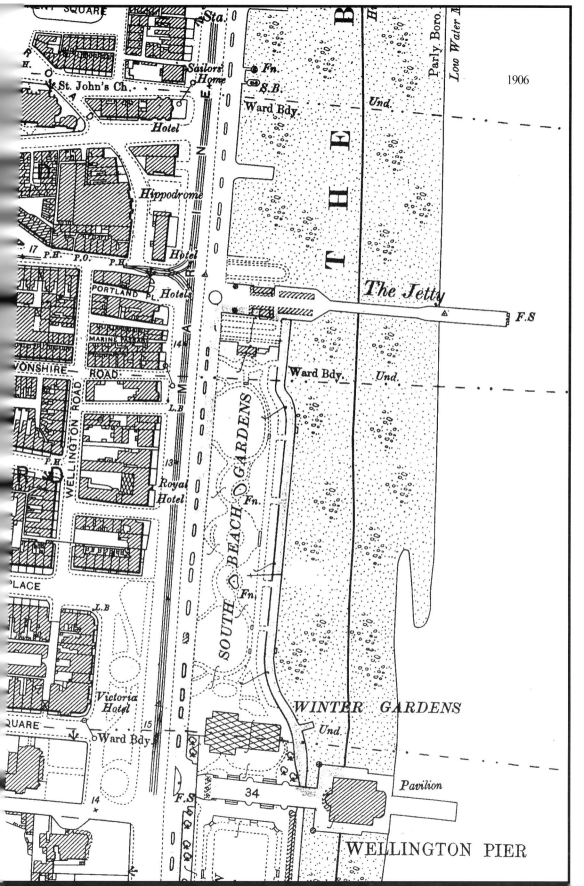

1906

The Jetty

F.S

THE B

Low Water

Parly. Boro.

Und.

Ward Bdy.

Fn.

S.B.

Sailors' Home

St. John's Ch.

Sta.

Hotel

Hippodrome

Hotel

P.H.   P.O.   P.H.

PORTLAND PL   Hotels

MARINE PARADE

DEVONSHIRE   ROAD

WELLINGTON   ROAD

L.B

P.H.

Royal Hotel

Victoria Hotel

L.B

PLACE

SQUARE

Ward Bdy

SOUTH   BEACH   GARDENS

Fn.

Fn.

Ward Bdy.   Und.

WINTER   GARDENS

Und.

Pavilion

34

F.S

WELLINGTON PIER

17

14

13

15

14

32.   A 1905/6 car is here seen at the terminus in 1931. In 1927 a new entrance to the Pavilion was constructed in a matching art nouveau style. Among the attractions on offer are military band concerts including one by the Black Watch. (Philip Standley coll.)

33.   Car 34 of the 1907 batch seems almost marooned on the Wellington Pier terminal stub in 1932. The wide carriageway southwards marks the line of a tramway extension to the South Denes. Had this and another extension along the North Denes been built, a 3½ mile/5.6km continuous seaside tramway would have been the result. The column visible in the distance between lamp posts (left) is the Nelson Monument. This is 144 feet high/43.8m and was completed in 1819; ten years before work began on London's Trafalgar Square. (M.J.O'Connor/ National Tramway Museum)

'BACK OF THE TOWN'
St Peters Road, Fishwharf and King Street

34.   We retrace our steps northward and turn west into St Peters Road to find track and overhead but no trams. Only intermittently was this installation put to use. This picture was probably taken shortly before it was removed in 1923. In the distance is the tower of what was then St Peter's Church and is now the Greek Orthodox Church of St. Spyridon. (Len Vincent coll.)

Ta 8897

Gt. Yarmouth Corp. Tramways
and Motor Bus Services

Outwards		Rewards
1		10
2	2½d	9
3		8
4		7
5		6
6		5
7		4
8		3
9		2
10		1

This Ticket must be retained for Inspection, and given up on demand. Available for Car and journey on which issued. Subject to the Corporation Bye-laws and Regulations.

PUNCH & TICKET CO. LONDON, N1

35. No pictures of trams south of St Peters Road were available for publication. However we see here one of a second batch of three ex-London General 'B' type buses purchased by the Corporation in 1925. The scene is the Fishwharf terminus. On the off-side top deck panels, would-be patrons were urged to 'Travel by Tram'! In the background, the entrance (right) and ventilator cowls (left) of the Corporation power station can be seen. The facade resembled a nineteeth century chapel. (First Bus/Norfolk Record Office)

36. Cars reached the Fishwharf via two blind bends. This two aspect (red and green) signal light box was therefore installed in Southgates Road as part of the 1926 reconstruction scheme. The lights were connected to skates in the overhead wire which were activated by the passage of a tram trolley wheel. Yarmouth Stores Ltd, outside whose store the signal was sited, supplied uniforms to the Great Yarmouth and Lowestoft tramway systems. In the present day, they supply crew jackets to the East Anglia Transport Museum. (Colin Tooke coll.)

37.   A distant tram draws us into the placid elegance of Edwardian King Street. Note the short bracket arms supporting two wires; one for each direction. Also, the nearest traction pole is doubling as a lamp post. Today, the tranquility is gone. The Yarmouth Way relief road has shaved off part of St George's Church yard (to the right) before plunging towards South Quay, thankfully just avoiding the elegant curved bay on the left. (Colin Tooke coll.)

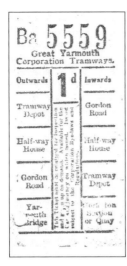

Ba **5559**
Great Yarmouth
Corporation Tramways.

Outwards	**1** d	Inwards
Tramway Depot		Gordon Road
Half-way House		Half-way House
Gordon Road		Tramway Depot
Yarmouth Bridge		Fish Wharf or Quay

38.   Car 11 is here seen in the stretch of King Street between Rows 90 and 93 in the early 1920s. The tram is almost certainly making for the Fish Wharf as the line along St Peter's Road would be on the point of being lifted. The bland functionalism of the 1940s and 1950s has since replaced many buildings to the left, but this street retains much character, particularly at first floor level.
(First Bus/Norfolk Record Office)

39. Car 13 passes briefly in King Street on its passage from Regent Road and into Regent Street on the 'back route' to Vauxhall Station from Wellington Pier. The date is 1903 or 1904 and summer time, judging by the policeman's white helmet and the ladies' blouses. (Peter Larter coll.)

40.   In this first storey view of King Street in the 1920s, overhead fittings can be seen at eye level while two trams pass at the Market Place corner. A 1902 car is heading north and a 1905 car making for Wellington Pier. (A.D.Packer coll.)

REGENT STREET,
QUAYS AND VAUXHALL STATION

41.   In this 1902 scene, car 13 has just entered Regent Street from Hall Quay. Like its London name-sake, Regent Street was a planned thoroughfare and built in 1813 to alleviate congestion in narrower streets. A combination of bracket arm and span wire 'pull offs' maintains the curvature of the overhead wires past the Town Hall (right). (Basil Gowen coll.)

42.	This is a fascinating depiction of passengers boarding one of the coastal paddle steamers at Hall Quay. Of these, the most famous were the Belle Steamers, but this is one of the General Steam Navigation Company's vessels, possibly the *Mavis*. In the background can be seen Press's High Mill, which was taken down in 1905. However, this neither authenticates nor dates the picture as the publisher has indulged in more than a little 'photo montage' to add to its appeal. The three window trams have been 'imported' from two unknown systems and placed on the quayside standard gauge tracks! Overhead wires and traction poles have also been 'provided'. In actuality, the tram tracks ran nearer to the shelter in the foreground. (National Tramway Museum coll.)

43.	Hall Quay is seen here in the early 1920s with the heavy municipal architecture of the Town Hall behind. Five forms of transport associated with Great Yarmouth can be seen. On the left, two landaus wait. In the centre, a 1905 tram is drawn up alongside a charabanc. To the right, a railway van stands on the standard gauge quayside tramway. Berthed by the quay is the *Southtown*, one of the double ended steamers on the ferry service to Gorleston. (National Tramway Museum coll.)

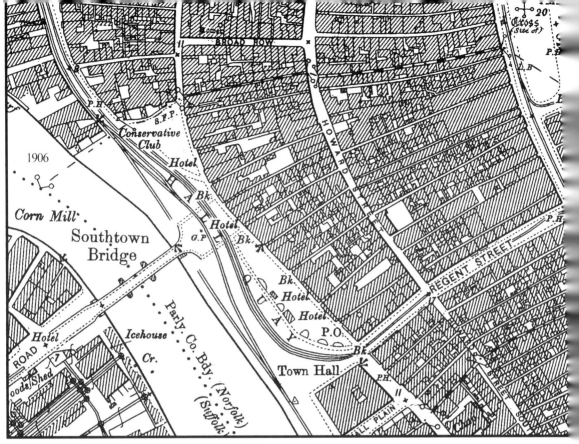

44.   A 1902 car is making its way across Hall Quay on its way to Vauxhall Station; in an autumn when the harbour was packed with herring fishing craft including many from Scottish ports. The cohabitation between the electric tramway (left) and the standard gauge quayside line in the foreground would have been quite complex had tram tracks been laid across Haven Bridge (right). (National Tramway Museum coll.)

45.   On North Quay, the electric tramway ran parallel with the Yarmouth Extension Railway, or harbour tramway. This connected Vauxhall Station to the quayside and a number of sidings over a distance of about a mile and a half. An extension in 1882 connected Beach Station to this network. Steam replaced horse power in 1884. Diesel shunters took over completely in 1955 and worked on until closure in 1975. Steam tram engine 68219 (LNER class J70) is here seen at the southern end of North Quay in the 1950s. The antiquity of the locomotive and of the steam yacht by the opposite river bank combine to evoke earlier days. (Stations UK)

46.   An unidentified 1902 car stands on the Vauxhall Staion terminal stub before World War I. A double tram track, a single line connection to the quayside tramway and the roadway shared Vauxhall Bridge, a bow string girder structure just out of the picture to the right. The tram track then became single before crossing and then running parallel to the harbour line. Vauxhall is now Great Yarmouth's only rail station. The tram service ended in 1929 and the Italienate station house gave way to a more modern structure in 1961. (Colin Tooke coll.)

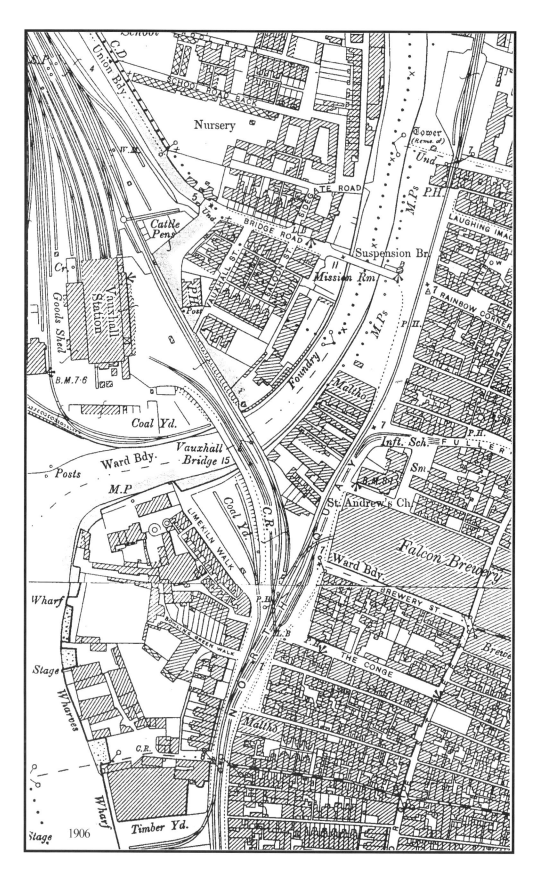

TOWN CENTRE TO CAISTER

47.   Latterly, the Caister service terminated in King Street in winter. On a very damp day in 1932, car 51 has arrived on what remains of the King Street track after the closure of the Fishwharf line in 1924. The terminal stub on Church Plain (see following picture) was removed at the same time. A single deck bus from the Fishwharf can be seen in the background heading for the Market Place. (Dr. Hugh Nicol/National Tramway Museum)

48.   We now briefly cover some ground already explored. Car 16 is here seen passing the terminal stub for the Caister service which was put in on Church Plain in 1907. The driver of the horse conveyance obviously considers that prossesion is nine tenths of the law and may, in any case, have a prior claim to this pitch (see picture 6). (First Bus/ Norfolk Record Office)

49.   In the absence of any photographs of trams or tracks on the long northward straight from Newtown, we arrive at the southern edge of Caister. The overhead for a passing loop is spread between two side poles, one of which supports feeder cables and a section switch. The 9 inch/228mm white bands on the poles were to aid visibility in the absence of street lighting. The wider band on the pole in the centre of the picture indicated a passenger stop. (Basil Gowen coll.)

50.   A tram trundles southward in about 1907, through an enlarging village which is still trim, tidy and tranquil. The passage of time and modern holiday traffic have since eroded these charms. But even the Edwardian scene was not without its perils. "Don't move, sir, or......"
(Basil Gowen coll.)

51.   Car 31 waits in the last passing loop for another car which has just set off from the terminus, a few yards beyond the loop. This view almost certainly dates from 1907 when the service to Caister was inaugurated. (Philip Standley coll.)

52.   Civic dignitaries, including the mayor, are here attending the formal opening of the Caister line on 16th May 1907. Behind the tram is a newly purchased tower wagon, presumably in attendance on a "just in case" basis. The driver, probably an inspector, adopts a military pose in anticipation of the return journey to Newtown, while local lads are keen to get a look in. (Colin Tooke coll.)

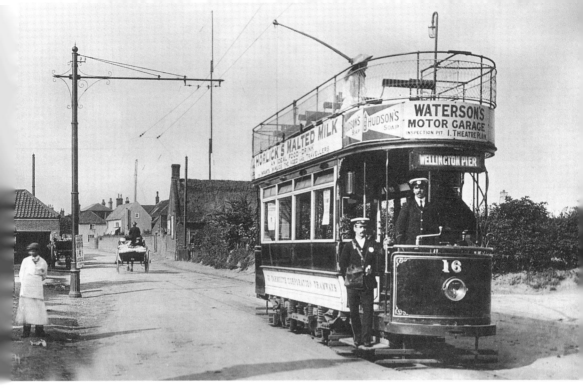

53.   The fine study of car 16 at the Caister terminus was taken in the early days of the service. The tail end of the overhead is held under tension by two side poles. The rural character of the surroundings was to change markedly in the following quarter century. (Basil Gowen coll.)

54.   The same location seen in the previous picture is depicted here from another angle. Car 33 awaits departure in the middle of the road which continues invitingly beyond. The sign by the white roofed cottage reads "E. Hewitt - wheelwright and coach builder". The site is now a double glazing sales office facing a car showroom on the opposite corner. The gentle ambience has gone. (Philip Standley coll.)

55.   The Caister terminus was moved to a kerbside position in 1924. In this 1932 view, motor vehicles are becoming evident and the surroundings more suburban. It would seem that the crew of car 3 have left it in haste without swinging the trolley, probably to attend to something urgent during their brief layover. (M.J. O'Connor/National Tramway Museum)

56. Again in 1932, car 15 waits in the Caister terminal stub. In the 25 years since picture 53 was taken, the 'arts and crafts' style Council Hall has been built as has a row of houses adjacent to it. The door of Camplings shop conjures a momentary illusion of a driver's windscreen which would have been an asset on such a wet day. (Dr Hugh Nicol/National Tramway Museum)

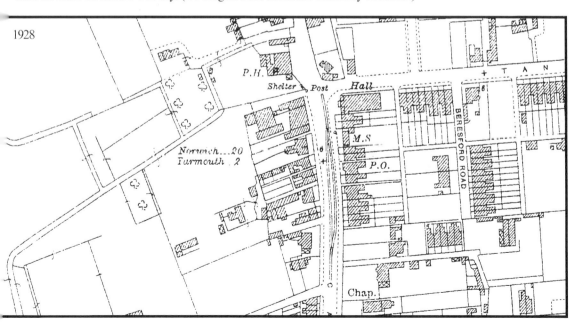

57.   This depicts the opening of the first street tramway; not only in Gorleston but in the whole of East Anglia on 25th March 1875. A local, artist interpreted the scene on Feathers Plain, Gorleston; a long awaited event as the first rail of the standard gauge (4ft 8½ins/1435mm) line had been laid in October 1872. The service offered a second class fare of 2d for the journey to Southtown. For an additional 1d, a first class fare allowed use of the inner most seats and additional straw to keep the feet warm! (Norfolk Heritage Centre)

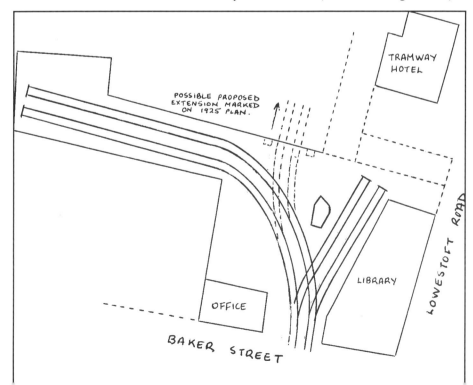

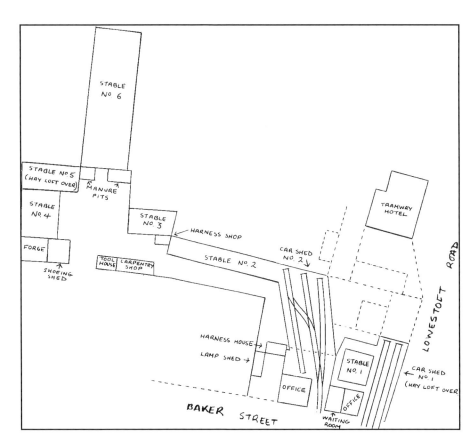

STABLE No 6

STABLE No 5
(HAY LOFT OVER)

MANURE PITS

STABLE No 4

STABLE No 3

FORGE

SHOEING SHED

TOOL HOUSE

CARPENTRY SHOP

HARNESS SHOP

STABLE No 2

CAR SHED No 2

TRAMWAY HOTEL

LOWESTOFT ROAD

HARNESS HOUSE

LAMP SHED

STABLE No 1

CAR SHED No 1 (HAY LOFT OVER)

OFFICE

OFFICE

WAITING ROOM

BAKER STREET

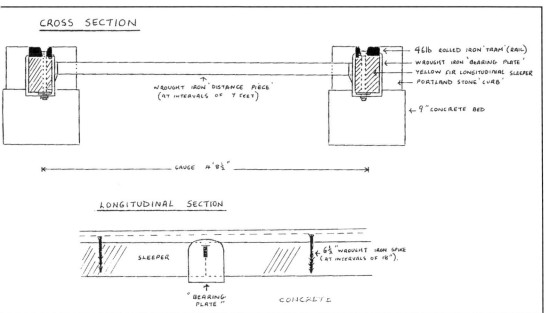

CROSS SECTION

← 46 lb ROLLED IRON TRAM (RAIL)
← WROUGHT IRON BEARING PLATE
← YELLOW FIR LONGITUDINAL SLEEPER
← PORTLAND STONE CURB

← 9" CONCRETE BED

WROUGHT IRON DISTANCE PIECE
(AT INTERVALS OF 7 FEET)

|← GAUGE 4' 8½" →|

LONGITUDINAL SECTION

SLEEPER

6½" WROUGHT IRON SPIKE
(AT INTERVALS OF 18").

"BEARING PLATE"

CONCRETE

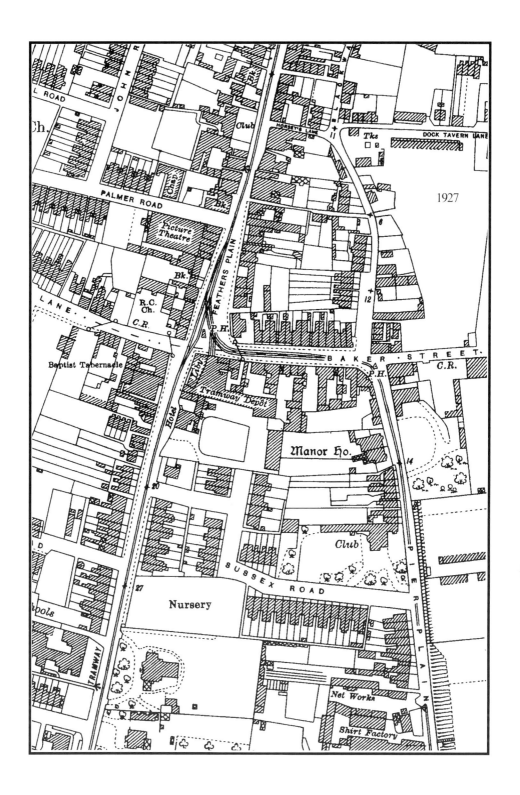

58.   It is June 1905 at Feathers Plain and the era of horse traction is ending. In the intervening years, the horse tram line had been reconstructed to 3ft 6ins gauge and equipped with newer cars. In the background, one of the replacing electric cars hovers outside the new depot. Contrary to the caption above the stairs, patrons of horse traction can expect a stately passage to Southtown only. (National Tramway Museum coll.)

59.   The 1882 horse car line reached Brush Quay via Englands Lane and Pier Walk. Here one of the cars turns into Lowestoft Road from Englands Lane with an additional ("cockey" or "trace") horse attached to assist against the gradient. Electric cars took a different route because of the narrowness of the lane. The theatre bill over the car canopy dates this picture as September 1891 or May 1897. (Author's coll.)

60.   From the lighthouse tower, we see a horse tram at the Brush Quay terminus about 1902. The steamer *Cobholm* on the ferry service from Hall Quay Great Yarmouth is moored close by. Passengers in their Sunday finery have made use of tickets offering outward journey by boat and return by tram or vice versa. (Colin Tooke coll.)

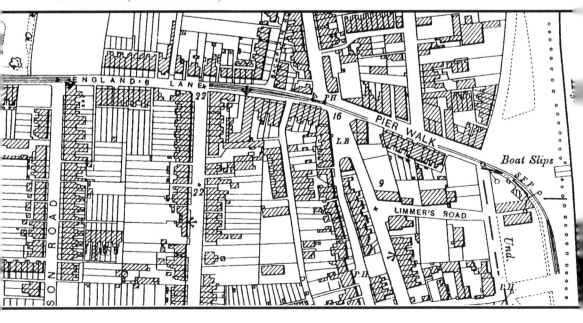

61.   Back at Feathers Plain, we see the opening of the electric car service on 4th July 1905. The Mayor, Alderman Mayo, is honorary driver of car 17 (destined to be Gorleston's last tram) which is turning towards Baker Street. The tracks heading left lead to Lowestoft Road. The site of Bucklands is now occupied by a bank. (Philip Standley coll.)

62.   Still on opening day at Feathers Plain, car 18 takes the new route to Beach Terminus via Baker Street. In the background, car 17, driven by Alderman Mayo, can be seen entering Pier Plain. Some of the bystanders view the photographer with consternation. (Brian Ollington coll.)

63.   From Baker Street, the track turns into Pier Plain - curiously named as it is a lane, not a plain and is not adjacent to a pier! This 1905 view shows car 26 passing a handcart belonging to Gorleston Laundry. (A.D.Packer coll.)

64.   Car 25 has passed the original terminus on Brush Quay (now alternatively styled Quay Road) and has reached the lighthouse from which picture 60 was taken. Gorleston lighthouse displayed a fixed red light for the guidance of vessels entering the river. The date is 1905 as the tram's destination box has not been moved to below the canopy. (A.D.Packer coll.)

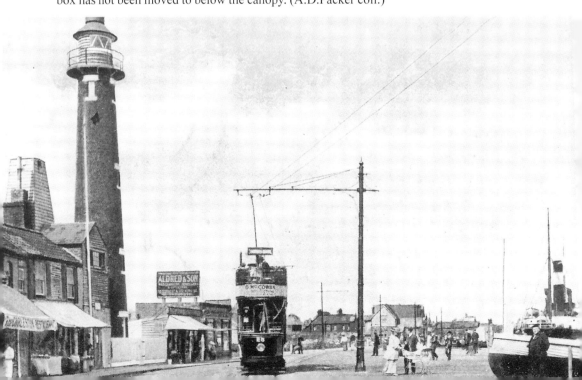

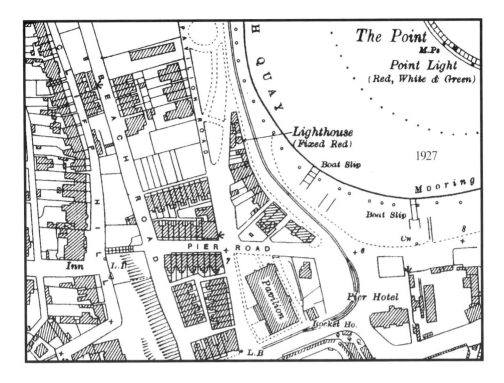

65.   Further along Brush Quay and beyond the lighthouse was the winter terminus for the electric cars. This could be a bleak and wind27thswept location. Beyond the tram, smoke from a steam drifter heading out to sea darkens an already grey sky. (Lens of Sutton)

66.   In this aerial view, probably from the 1920s, a figure can be seen hurrying to catch the tram - far right. The large building top right is the Pavilion, the Corporation's first venture into indoor entertainment. The summer terminus is by the awnings. Much of the gardens opposite are now covered by another entertainment venue, the Ocean Rooms. (Colin Tooke coll.)

67.   Back almost to Feathers Plain we meet car 18 entering Lowestoft Road. On the corner is the 1905 library building, standing on part of the site of the horse tram depot. The distinctive clock has two faces and is set at an angle in order to be seen from four directions. A modern library and clock now stand on broadly the same site. (Colin Tooke coll.)

68. Further along Lowestoft Road, car 18 passes the corner of Nile Road and some of the more opulent Gorleston houses on the other side of the road. These were still being built when the electric tramway opened in 1905. (National Tramway Museum coll.)

69. The Gorleston Station terminus was just before the corner of Springfield Road. In this 1905 view, car 26 is brand new and carrying no advertising. The driver is posed in action mode against the direction of the trolley, a bad example to the young would-be tram drivers in attendance. The end of the overhead is held in tension by a bracket arm set at an angle. (A.D.Packer coll.)

70.   Car 19 is seen here at Gorleston Station terminus, looking south and in winter. The crew have darkened caps and the driver is wearing at least one pair of thick gloves. The bridge over the railway can be seen in the background. The railway was a relative latecomer being opened in 1903. It closed in 1970. The station itself was in a cutting through which a rather angry stretch of the Gorleston relief road now runs. (Brian Ollington coll.)

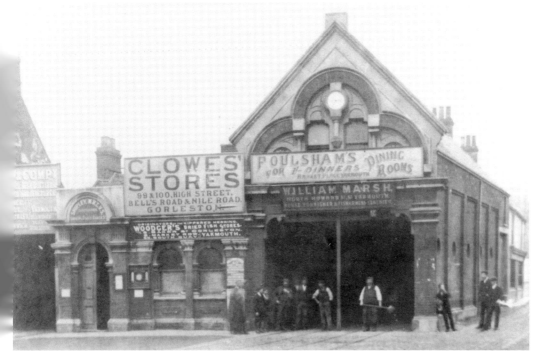

71.   The facade of the 1882 horse tram depot in Feathers Plain had the look of a Chapel about it. The door (left) was to a waiting room while a single track entry to a further depot is left of that. The combined depot was home to 10 trams, 7 horse buses and 68 horses. The gentleman with the shovel was kept busy. (First Bus/Norfolk Record Office)

72.   The need for a new electric car depot in 1905 coincided with funding from the Carnegie Foundation for a new public library. The two were, therefore, contained within one new building on the site of the old horse car depot. The library opened onto Lowestoft Road (right) while the depot access was through the rather grand portal in Baker Street. The depot roof was already off when this pre-demolition picture was taken in the 1970s. (P. Larter coll.)

FEATHERS PLAIN TO SOUTHTOWN

73.　　We now set out from Feathers Plain for our journey along the tramway main line. Car 21 will pass in front of us en route to Gorleston Beach and past the depot approach tracks in the foreground. A procession of horse drawn conveyances crosses the plain and enters Palmer Road. The construction of public toilets and other amenities has since deprived Gorleston of this uncluttered open space. (Brian Ollington coll.)

74.　　Seen from the High Street end of Feathers Plain, car 19 is about to pass another car proceeding from Gorleston Beach. The passing loop is just behind the horse drawn trap. Lowestoft Road can be seen receding into the distance on the right of the picture. (Basil Gowen coll.)

75.   Just a little further into High Street, a horse car is about to enter Feathers Plain past the corner of Palmer Road. This tranquil scene is probably from the late 1890s. No flourishing gardens face the High Street today. (Colin Tooke coll.)

76.   Car 20 of the new electric age has ushered in remarkably little other change if this scene and the previous one are compared. The nearer building that the tram is passing to our left is the old Post Office. Next, the halls of the Oddfellows and Salvation Army stand adjacent. (Basil Gowen coll.)

77.   On a quiet afternoon in May 1892, a horse car trundles northward in Gorleston High Street. Lack of patronage affords time for the conductor to pass the time of day with a policeman who shares the platform. A row of shops, including Boots the Chemist, now stand where trees and shrubs were once someone's pride.
(Norfolk Heritage Centre)

78.   Two horse cars pass at the appropriately named "Halfway House" hostelry. This was buil in 1882, the year the second horse tram line wa opened, and replaced an earlier tavern, the 'Guardian Angel' on the same site. Stables fo non tramway travellers are provided via the arch The shelter beyond is for tramway passengers All this was swept away in 1968 to make way fo a dual carriageway. The gabled gas works building, seen between the cars, serves as a reference point by which to plot this location in the present day. (Basil Gowen coll.)

79.   The destination of car 24 sounds almost apologetic but there is no expression of contrition on the faces of the crew. This location by "Halfway House" could have become a tramway junction if plans for a transporter bridge across the Yare had been pursued. This would have linked the Fishwharf with Gas House Quay, near to the gas holders seen to the left. (Colin Tooke coll.)

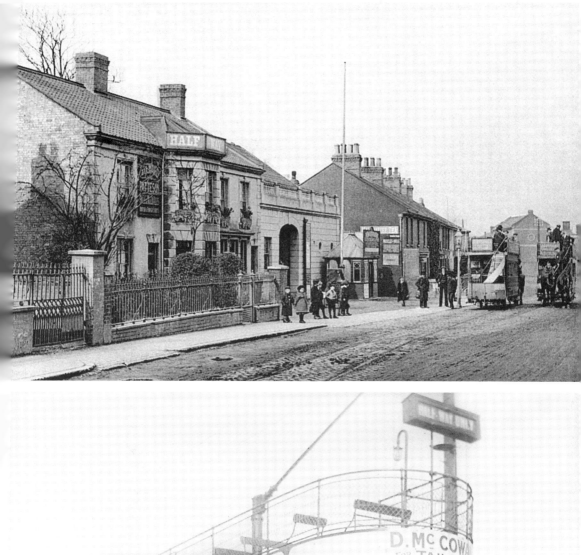

80.	Car 20 is here seen proceeding north in Southtown Road alongside Bollard Quay. The steam drifters and tall masts now live only in the past, while the promising young trees have given way to a concrete flood wall. A little further on to the left was the access to the original horse tram depot. (Colin Tooke coll.)

81.	Car 21, bound for Gorleston Beach, is stopped in Southtown Road opposite the corner of Albany Road and is running late. Another car bound for Gorleston Station is coming up behind so the driver is looking back in anticipation of the conductor's ring of the bell before moving off briskly. (Author's coll.)

82.   Southtown and Cobholm in particular have had to live with the possibility of flooding, although recent measures have reduced the risk considerably. Top deck passengers of this horse car stand for a better view of the 1905 spectacle in Southtown Road between Anson Road (left) and Portland Lane (right). (Philip Standley coll.)

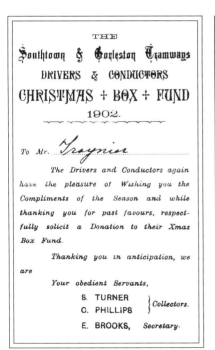

THE

Southtown & Gorleston Tramways

DRIVERS & CONDUCTORS

CHRISTMAS ✦ BOX ✦ FUND

1902.

To Mr. _Traynier_

The Drivers and Conductors again have the pleasure of Wishing you the Compliments of the Season and while thanking you for past favours, respectfully solicit a Donation to their Xmas Box Fund.

Thanking you in anticipation, we are

Your obedient Servants,

S. TURNER ⎱
C. PHILLIPS ⎰ Collectors.

E. BROOKS, Secretary.

Great Yarmouth Corporation Tramways.

TIME TABLE ALTERATION.

On and after Friday, 26th September, 1919, and until further notice,

The Car Service will be as follows:

YARMOUTH SECTION.

(timetable details)

GORLESTON SECTION.

(timetable details)

Whilst exercising every care to ensure correct running of the Cars, the Corporation will not be responsible for any detention or delay which may unavoidably arise.

NOTICE.

COUNTERFEIT AND FOREIGN COINS

Proceedings will be taken against any Passenger endeavouring to pass Counterfeit or other Coins not in circulation in payment of the Tram Fare.

Tramways Offices, Caister Road.
23rd Sept., 1919.

FREDK. L. TURNER, General Manager.

83. This stretch of Southtown Road exudes gentility and respectability in this Edwardian view in which the tramway installation seems polite and orderly. Industry in the shape of large timber wharves and warehouses is not far away. Today, St Mary's Church (pinnacles left) still manages to maintain dignity in increasingly commercial surroundings. (Basil Gowen coll.)

────────►

84. This aerial photograph, probably from 1927 shows Southtown Road (bottom) and Bridge Road (left). Tracks from Southtown Station cross the tramway on the level to reach the goods depot. A tram waits in the terminal stub (mid left) while other cars on the Vauxhall Station service pass on Hall Quay beyond Southtown Bridge. Work is progressing on piers for the temporary bridge in advance of the replacement of the 1854 structure seen here still in use. (Mike Lawrence coll.)

────────►

85. Round the corner into Bridge Road we find car 23 waiting in the kerbside siding that was laid in 1922. Hitherto, the track had ended in the middle of the road, causing congestion and some danger in the increasing levels of motor traffic. (Colin Tooke coll.)

86.   Adjacent to the Southtown terminus, potential passengers are encouraged to sample the attributes of "Picturesque Gorleston-on-Sea - Yarmouth's charming suburb". Much is made of the spectacle of the fishing fleet at the harbour mouth. (Colin Tooke coll.)

87.   Three decorated electric cars stand at the Southtown Bridge terminus on the occasion of the ceremonial opening of the electrified line on 4th July 1905. The driver of car 17 is the Mayor, Alderman Mayo, who seems to be familiarising himself with the handbrake rachet and 'dog'
. The thatched building is one of two ice houses. One still stands and is the only recorded surviving commercial ice house. (National Tramway Museum coll.)

88.　　In 1927, the decision was made to build a new bridge but without provision for a tramway. This effectively sealed the fate of car 25 and its fellows. In the background, the bridge works loom in this 1929 photograph. A billboard in the passenger shelter is headed 'Great Eastern Railway', six years after that railway became part of the LNER. (Dr Hugh Nicol/ National Tramway Museum)

CARS IN DISGUISES AND FANCY DRESS

89.   This First World War tank, seen on North Quay, is in fact a disguised tram being used as a platform to promote sale of National War Bonds in 1917. The tram must be gripped by a dual identity crisis as it carries a Yarmouth fishing craft registration number! 7 evidently signified good luck in the town's fishery circles. The tramway had its own telecommunication system. A telephone box can be seen just below 'cars stop here' on the traction column near to the policeman (left). (Basil Gowen coll.)

90.   Two cars stand bedecked on Feathers Plain together with the depot 'gardeners' who have brought their charges into 'bloom'. The occasion is the Gorleston Carnival of 1923. (Brian Ollington coll.)

91.   The *Pride of Gorleston* was launched for the 1924 carnival. It conveys a hint of what a Great Yarmouth car would have looked like with an enclosed top deck. The Brush company submitted drawings of top covers to the Corporation, probably more in hope than in expectation. (Colin Tooke coll.)

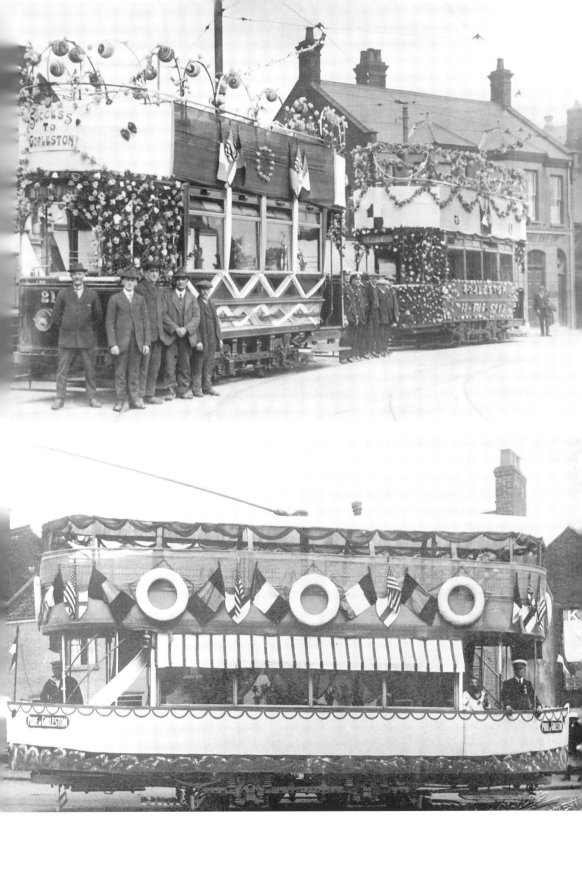

92.   Seen at the west end of Regent Road, this bedecked car carries the slogan "Success to Yarmouth's" at cantrail level and "Carnival 1923" more obscurely at the waist. The conductor is wearing a 'fez' which , at the time, would be humorously associated with the sale of naughty postcards and not tram tickets! (Colin Tooke coll.)

93.   This 1902 car, seen on the depot forecourt became a 'Viennese Houseboat' for the Yarmouth Carnival of 1924. In that year, the ancient swastika decoration could be applied in innocence. It had not yet been appropriated and reversed by dark forces. (First Bus/Norfolk Record Office)

94.   Two trams one each side of the river, operated as mobile advertisements for light bulbs. The subject here is car 34 or 35 and probably seen in Theatre Plain. The two blobs of light above are the upper deck illumination. (National Tramway Museum)

ROLLING STOCK

Standard Gauge 1875 Cars

East Anglian, then East Suffolk, then Yarmouth & Gorleston Tramway Companies (standard gauage - 4ft 8½ins). Very little information about these cars and only two photographs could be traced. These depict double deck cars with spiral ladders (as distinct from stairs) and "knifeboard" (back to back) top deck seats. These are to the design of Starbuck of Birkenhead and were probably built by them, although the design was copied by others. Cars of this type usually had india rubber block suspension and button-backed upholstery on the saloon seats. Seating capacity of such cars was usually 18 in the saloon and 22 on the "knifeboard". Three cars were already in stock when construction of the line commenced in 1872. These may have been the entire fleet, as the line had only one passing place.

Yarmouth and Gorleston Tramway Company 1842 Cars (narrow gauge 3ft 6ins).

These 10 identical cars were built by the Midland Carriage and Wagon Co of Shewsbury. They seated 24 inside on slatted wooden seats and 22 on a "knifeboard" on the top deck. No fleet numbers are obvious on photographs, but each car carried a licence number plate on the bulkhead. Circumstantial evidence suggests that the livery was mostly cream or yellow with red waist level panels.

Great Yarmouth Corporation Electric Cars (narrow gauge 3ft 6ins).

All of these cars were supplied by the Brush Electrical Engineering Co. of Loughborough and to that company's standard designs. Brush also supplied the 6 foot/1.8m wheelbase trucks and electrical equipment, including two 25hp motors for each car. All were open top double deckers with reversible 'garden' seats on the top deck. All had longitudinal slatted seats for 22 passengers in the lower saloon (except cars 32-35). The livery was maroon and cream, described as 'raspberry jam and custard'. The maroon was double-lined in gold and the cream singly in black. Lettering was gold shaded blue. The Borough arms was displayed midway along the waist panels.

1902 Cars 1-14

Features were seating for 27 passenger on the top deck and reversed (clockwise) stairs The four windows each side were radiused at th top corners. Service brakes and emergenc electric brakes were provided. The original Brus type A trucks were fitted with small leaf spring above each axle box. These trucks were modifie with coil springs and axle box bridles in 1909 t counteract harsh and bouncy riding.

Eight cars (numbers not known) were sen to Burton-on-Trent to augment war factory transport in 1918 but were returned unused. Al were rebuilt from 1923 onwards with normal (counterclockwise) stairs and with destination boxes resited below the canopies. Trucks were upgraded, three to AA specification with new frames, one with anti-galloping gear and the remainder (including 2, 3, 6, 7, 9) with conversion sets incorporating wide wing axelboxes. Car 9 later received a type AA truck, probably from a car withdrawn in 1930. None of these cars operated on the Gorleston section.

1905 Cars 15-26 and 1906 27-31

These had normal stairs from the outset and type AA trucks in which the vices of type A had been designed out. At 28 feet/8.5m, they were 6 inches longer than the earlier cars. Saloon interiors and the top deck railings were both higher, the latter to conform with new regulations. The railings also carried a wire mesh to a design peculiar to Brush cars of the period. The top decks seated 32. The 1906 cars had destination boxes fixed below the canopies, the 1905 batch being altered to conform in 1906. These and the subsequent batch of cars had electrical service braking.

Cars 17 to 28 were initially allocated to Gorleston Depot and the remainder to Caister Road. 15 and 16 were later transferred to Gorleston. Following the Gorleston closure in 1930, numbers 15, 16, 19, 20 and 24 replaced more run down cars on the Yarmouth section. Other temporary transfers also occurred. These cars were rebuilt in the 1920s but with no obvious change to their appearance.

907 Cars 32-35

These cars brought the fleet up to strength for the new Caister service and differed from earlier cars in three respects. Downstairs, 18 transverse reversible seats were provided but were quickly replaced by the standard longitudinal arrangement. On top, there was a curved seat, for 4 passengers, over each canopy instead of reversible seating for 6. The saloon windows were set in separate frames that could be lowered. None of these cars crossed the river to Gorleston.

Withdrawal Dates

These cannot be determined conclusively as many cars were stored long after they ceased to run. There was certainly some cannibalisation and maybe some re-instatement, car 35 being a possible example. The following cars were disposed of or scrapped before or following the Gorleston closure in 1930: 1, 4, 5, 8, 11-18, 21-23, 25-28, 33, 35. Cars 2, 3, 6, 7, 9, 10, 19, 20, 24, 29-32, and 34 went by or following final closure in 1933.

1882 Horse Car

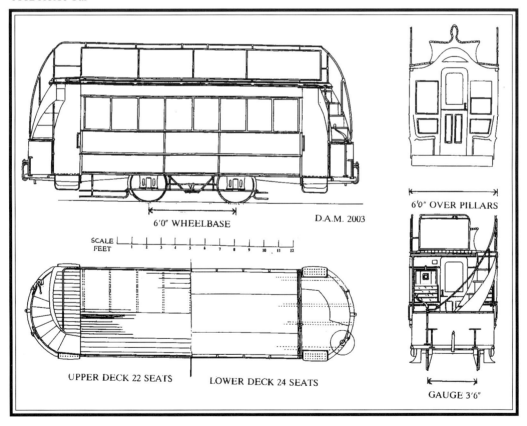

6'0" WHEELBASE

D.A.M. 2003

SCALE FEET

6'0" OVER PILLARS

UPPER DECK 22 SEATS   LOWER DECK 24 SEATS

GAUGE 3'6"

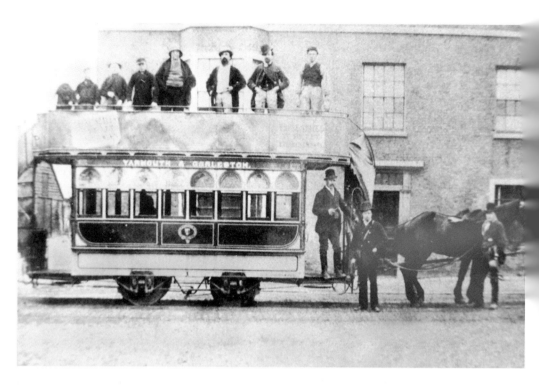

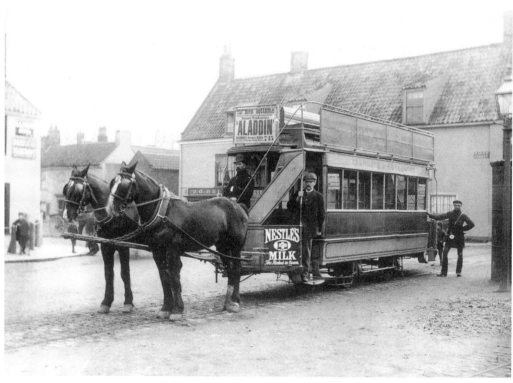

95.   One of the Starbuck designed cars of the original standard gauge Yarmouth & Gorleston line
is seen here with an intriguing group of characters on the top deck. Originally, the spiral ladders and
top deck rails were open (see picture 57). What appear to be canvas screens have here been added as
draught-proofing and decency panels. (Norfolk Heritage Centre)

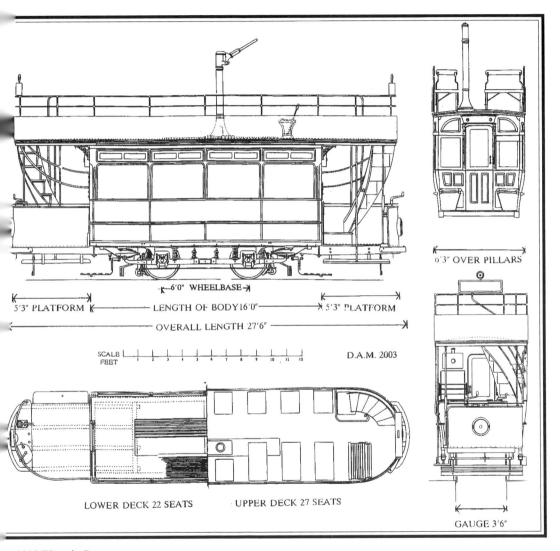

6'3" OVER PILLARS

6'0" WHEELBASE

5'3" PLATFORM ⊢——— LENGTH OF BODY 16'0"——→ 5'3" PLATFORM

OVERALL LENGTH 27'6"

SCALE FEET 1 2 3 4 5 6 7 8 9 10 11 12   D.A.M. 2003

LOWER DECK 22 SEATS   UPPER DECK 27 SEATS

GAUGE 3'6"

1902 Electric Car

96.   One of the Midland built horse cars for the 3ft 6ins gauge line is seen here at Feathers Plain
Gorleston in 1897. Although working on narrower track, these cars were larger than their predecessors.
Having more satisfactory track to run on, also meant that they lasted rather longer. Great Yarmouth
Corporation took over and ran the remaining serviceable cars for four months in 1905 while the new
electrified Gorleston line was being installed. (Percy Trett coll.)

97.   Car 8 of the 1902 batch of Corporation electric cars is seen here at Caister Road Depot in company with a trio of dog fanciers, probably in 1903. The car is in almost original condition apart from the illuminated stencil route indicator boxes which soon replaced the boards on the fenders (see pictures 21, 24 & 41). Features of note are the single bar lifeguards, fixed platform steps and radiussed top corners to the saloon windows. The lower (rocker) body panels are unlettered. The Corporation Tramways title was applied in 1905. (Brian Ollington coll.)

98.   Car 7 was photographed at the same location in 1909 when Board of Trade approval was given for improved lifeguards designed by Mr Wildbur, the car shed foreman. These had an enlarged gate with three bars. To enable them to swing freely, retractable platform steps were fitted. That seen in the picture is in the raised position while the lifeguard trays have been dropped. By this time, the operator's title has been applied to the bodyside. The original springing arrangement of the Brush type 'A' truck can be seen. In the roof of the depot is the troughing; a means of obviating the dewirement of the trolley which might otherwise become entangled in the roof trusses. (Brian Ollington coll.)

99.   Car 1 is here seen in 1905, when silver braid was added to crews' uniforms. The stencil box route indicator was later replaced by the roller blind type. The offset position of the trolley mast is well portrayed in this picture. (Basil Gowen coll.)

100.   Car 9 of the same batch is seen in 1929. Changes as a result of the 1923 rebuilding programme are evident, including normal (clockwise) stairs, revised destination display and removal of the Board of Trade oil lamp from the bulkhead. A new fender with towing slot has been fitted. Earlier changes are the revised livery to the bulkhead and the retractable step. The centre stancheon has been cranked to the platform edge to accommodate this. The conductor is believed to be Mr. Jimmy Errington who regularly walked from his Northgate Street home to join the first shift from Gorleston Depot. He later transferred to Caister Road depot and to a much shorter walk. (Dr H.A.Whitcombe - Science Museum Science & Society Picture Library)

left) 101. This 1902 car (believed to be number 1) is posed on Caister Road Depot forecourt to illustrate features of the 1923 rebuilding. In addition to those already noted are the new wide wing axleboxes and revised springing. The diagonal braces at each end of the truck were marketed as 'anti-galloping gear' and designed to smooth out the pitching motion of a short wheelbase car. The fitment in this case was evidently an experiment which failed to satisfy as only the one set was purchased. (Author's coll.)

(lower left) 102. The final condition of the 1902 batch of cars is illustrated as a proud crew pose with an immaculate number 2. The car is fresh from what was almost certainly its last repaint. (Colin Tooke coll.)

(above) 103. Car 24 of the 1905 batch is here seen as brand new. The platform step is raised and the lattice gate, a feature of these cars when new, is closed at the driver's end. On the canopy is the intruction 'Swing the pole this side' - to avoid the twisting of the trolley cable in the mast. Conversion kits incorporating spring contacts were later available to overcome this inconvenience. The 1905 cars introduced a revised livery with maroon carried up to the top of the bulkhead and decorative motifs applied to the lining corners. (Brian Ollington coll.)

104.   In 1906, car 24 and its contemporaries had their destination boxes fixed under the canopies. This was a much neater arrangement bringing the handles within the reach of the driver and away from tinkering hands upstairs. The rotatable disc remained aloft, albeit a little lower. This was specific to the Gorleston cars and displayed either red for Gorleston Beach bound cars or green for those terminating at Gorleston Station. These colours corresponded to those displayed by the bulkhead oil lamp at night. (Brian Ollington coll.)

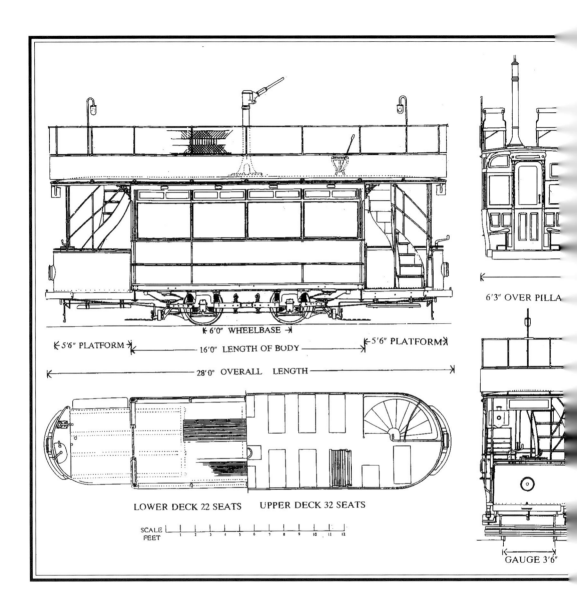

6'3" OVER PILLA..

6'0" WHEELBASE

5'6" PLATFORM

16'0" LENGTH OF BODY

5'6" PLATFORM

28'0" OVERALL LENGTH

LOWER DECK 22 SEATS   UPPER DECK 32 SEATS

SCALE
FEET

GAUGE 3'6"

105.   Car 15 typifies the 1905/1906 batches from both sides of the river, as seen in their later years. The location is the Southtown terminus about 1929. This car originally ran in Great Yarmouth. It was transferred following the Gorleston closure in 1930. These and the subsequent and final batch had scoop ventilators just below the cantrail. This was not a feature of the 1902 cars which were the only batch to have the radiused top window corners.

(Dr Hugh Nicol/ National Tramway Museum)

106.   One of the final (1907) delivery of four cars is seen here in the early 1930s. It is almost certainly car 34, the only one of this batch known to have been lettered "Gt Yarmouth Corporation Transport". The saloon windows of these cars were designed to be lowered in warm weather; hence the additional framing to the glazing. No photographs have been found showing this facility in use. On the top deck, a curved seat for four passengers was provided over each canopy. Inside, transverse reversible seats were provided for 18 passengers. This left a gangway of only 12¼ ins/311mm. Standard longitudinal seats were substituted within a year. (A.D.Packer)

107.   Cars from the first and final batches are here seen passing shortly after World War I. The 1902 cars, illustrated here by number 4, had lower top deck rails than those on succeeding batches which were so built to conform with new Board of Trade regulations implemented in 1904. (A.D.Packer coll.)

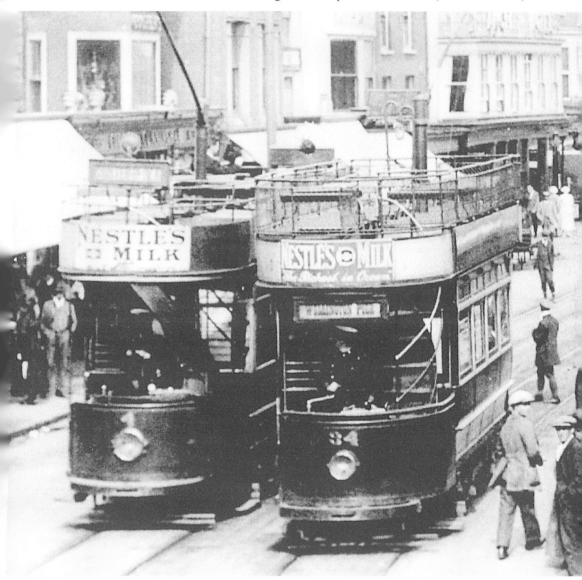

SOME TRAMWAY PEOPLE

108.   This staff photograph, dating from 1905 is, in fact, two photographs joined together. That to the left is of Yarmouth crews and maintenance men outside Caister Road Depot and against the backdrop of the municipal refuse destructor plant! The Gorleston contingent to the right have brought a glimpse of Church Lane with them. Both tramcars would have been brand new at the time. Given the diversity of tramway advertising, Horlicks should have been very pleased with the consistent message.
(First Bus/ Norfolk Record Office)

109.   This group of Gorleston crews was photographed outside the Feathers Plain Depot during Mr P.G. Campling's period of office as General Manager over the pivotal period from 1922 to 1930. Mr Campling is seated in the centre. The group includes seven former drivers of Gorleston horse trams, including Messrs Ward (front row-far left), Limmer (second row - second from left), Durrant (seated second row far right), Best (seated next to Durrant), Simmonds (standing - third row - second from left), Daws (third row - fifth from left), Tennant (on platform - far right). The Corporation offered superior terms of employment and recognised years of service with the horse tramways for pay and pensions. (Colin Tooke coll.)

110.   Car 32 and crew are here seen, all three smartly turned out. The lettering, lining and decorative livery features applied from 1905 are clearly portrayed. Driver's and conductor's double-breasted jackets carry their numbers on the shoulders and have leather covered cuffs. Each crew member wears a circular licence disc. Caps have summer white covers. In addition to his cash bag, the conductor is carrying a Williamson ticket punch. (Colin Tooke coll.)

AFTERMATH

111.   Workmen are seen removing tram tracks on Feathers Plain following the 1930 closure of the Gorleston system. A steamroller is breaking up the paving while cutting equipment is on hand to tackle the rails. Comparison with earlier views (73 in particular) will indicate the arrival [in 1914] of the Coliseum Cinema on the site of a row of small cottages. A row of shops can also be seen in what had been a front garden. The cinema was demolished in 1970. (Colin Tooke coll.)

112.   This is the nearest that Gorleston came to a steam tram though one is portrayed on the sign of the Tramway Hotel. Two redundant car bodies are here seen in Church Lane on their way to a new life as chalets at Caister Holiday Camp. A single deck bus harries from behind as if to make sure that they had gone. (Colin Tooke coll.)

113.   In the early 1930s, Caister Holiday Camp was literally a camp. Three forms of repose were on offer including more than 20 old trams; complete except for running gear. Fourteen of them are discernible in this photograph. This was the very first British holiday camp. It was set up in 1906 by Fletcher Dodd and based on socialist principles. (Colin Tooke coll.)

114.   Caister Holiday Camp Railway Halt on the M&GN line from Yarmouth Beach station is seen here in the 1930s and shortly after the new cafe was built. The two 1905/6 tram bodies represent station buildings. That to the left appears to be lettered Ladies Room and to have facilities provided at the further end. (Malcolm Banyer coll.)

115.   Of the car bodies not sold as holiday camp chalets, two ended their days on a farm adjacent to the Caister Road where they were photographed, probably in the late 1940s. These are known to be the bodies of cars 6 and 12, one of which was the ceremonial last car in December 1933. (East Anglia Transport Museum)

116.   Three Great Yarmouth tramway electrical section boxes can be seen at the East Anglia Transport Museum where two remain on duty. Regrettably, they do not provide power to any Great Yarmouth cars, all of which have escaped the preservation movement. (Author)

117.   This horse tram looks a little careworn as it awaits passengers on Feathers Plain in the closing days of horse traction in July 1905. In the nearer saloon window is a notice of the forthcoming sale of 60 horses, including the two seen here. Examples of names given to the tramway horses were Starchy, Prince, Cockrell, Ping Pong, Lopsy Popsy, and Smasher. The crew are wearing their British Electric Traction uniforms introduced in 1900. (Brian Ollington coll.)

In Loving Remembrance of the
YARMOUTH and GORLESTON HORSE TRAMS,

Which

succumbed on

July 4th, 1905

to an

Electric Shock.

Aged 30 Years.

Let not ambition mock their useful toil,
Their homely joys, and destiny obscure.

118.   Black-edged post cards were published to commem-
orate the passing away of the Gorleston to Southtown horse
trams. Not dissimilar cards incorporationg the "electric shock"
reference were produced to mark the end of horse traction on
a number of systems thoughout the country. In this particular
case, general electrocution seems to be assured by the
presence of so much flood water. (Basil Gowen coll.)

SEPTEMBER 26th, 1930.
GREAT YARMOUTH TRANSPORT DEPARTMENT.

TIME TABLE ALTERATION—GORLESTON SECTION.

On and after FRIDAY, September 26th, the TRAM SERVICE will be entirely Discontinued and substituted
by a BUS SERVICE which will be operated every 5 minutes between Theatre Plain and Gorleston-on-Sea.

Times of Departure as follows:—

BUSES LEAVE—	a.m.		p.m.	SUNDAYS.			
				a.m.			p.m.
Theatre Plain for Elmhurst via Church Road at 7.25	and every 16 min. until 10.55			9.25	and every 15 min. until		10.40
,, ,, ,, High Street ,, 7.35	,	15	, 11.10	9.35	,, 15 ,		10.35
,, Gor. Links ,, Church Road ,, 7.40	,	30	, 10.40	9.40	,, 30 ,		10.10
,, Gor. Beach ,, High Street ,, 7.45	,	15	, 10.45	9.30	,, 15 ,		10.30
BUSES LEAVE—	a.m.		p.m.	a.m.			p.m.
Elmhurst for Theatre Plain via Church Road at 7.45	,	30	, 11.15	9.45	and every 30 min. until		11.0
,, ,, ,, High Street ,, 7.55	,	15	, 11.30	9.55	,, 15 ,		10.55
Gor. Links ,, ,, ,, Church Road ,, 8.0	,	30	, 11.0	10.0	,, 30 ,		10.30
Gor. Beach ,, ,, ,, High Street ,, 8.5	,	16	, 11.5	9.50	,, 15 ,		10.50

EARLY MORNING SERVICE.

Until further notice, a SPECIAL BUS will leave as follows:—

Theatre Plain for Elmhurst at 6.10, 6.45, 7.15 a.m.   Elmhurst for Theatre Plain at 6.30, 7.0, 7.30 a.m.

Transport Office,
Caister Road.
September 20th.

H. A. BLACKBURN, Assoc. I.E.E., A.M. Inst., T.,
General Manager and Engineer.

GREAT YARMOUTH
Corporation Transport Department

Special Notice.

CAISTER (Tan Lane)
MARKET PLACE
AND
WELLINGTON PIER.

On and after FRIDAY, Dec. 15th,
THE

Tram Service

Between the above-mentioned points
will be

Superseded
BY
Motor Buses

Time Schedule and Fares will
remain as at Present.

H. A. BLACKBURN, M. INST. T., A.I.E.E.
General Manager and Engineer.

Transport Offices,
Caister Road, Great Yarmouth.
Dec. 6th, 1933.

JOHN BUCKLE, PRINTER, THEATRE PLAIN, GT. YARMOUTH.

9.   The lights are about to go out on the Gorleston trams on the night of 25th October 1930, although the closure had earlier been scheduled for September 26th. Car 17 is seen here at Southtown terminus from where it had been the first car in the opening procession of 1905. Conductor Read (with ticket punch by platform) was with number 17 on both of these occasions. Five of its fellows were transferred to Great Yarmouth Depot, but 17 was not so lucky and took enforced retirement. (First Bus/Norfolk Record Office)

20.   In 1933 came the ultimate 'adieu'. The last car (believed to be number 6 or number 12) is seen here outside Caister Road Depot, festooned with electric lights and bunting for the final run on 14th December. Two dimensional vases of flowers have been placed in two of the windows and the lower panels bear the new title "Gt Yarmouth Corporation Transport". The four tramwaymen of the 'old guard' seen here did not transfer to buses, but worked out their remaining years of service on depot duties. They are J.Denmark, W.A.Read, W.Read and J.Tennant. (First Bus/Norfolk Record Office)

MP Middleton Press

Easebourne Lane, Midhurst, W Sussex. GU29 9AZ Tel: 01730 813169 Fax: 01730 812601
Email: enquiries@middletonpress.fsnet.co.uk *If books are not available from your
local transport stockist, order direct with cheque, Visa or Mastercard, post free UK.*

BRANCH LINES

Branch Line to Allhallows
Branch Line to Alton
Branch Lines around Ascot
Branch Line to Ashburton
Branch Lines around Bodmin
Branch Line to Bude
Branch Lines around Canterbury
Branch Lines around Chard & Yeovil
Branch Line to Cheddar
Branch Lines around Cromer
Branch Line to the Derwent Valley
Branch Lines to East Grinstead
Branch Lines of East London
Branch Lines to Effingham Junction
Branch Lines around Exmouth
Branch Lines to Falmouth, Helston & St. Ives
Branch Line to Fairford
Branch Lines around Gosport
Branch Line to Hayling
Branch Lines to Henley, Windsor & Marlow
Branch Line to Hawkhurst
Branch Line to Ilfracombe
Branch Line to Kingsbridge
Branch Line to Kingswear
Branch Line to Lambourn
Branch Lines to Launceston & Princetown
Branch Lines to Longmoor
Branch Line to Looe
Branch Line to Lyme Regis
Branch Line to Lynton
Branch Lines around March
Branch Lines around Midhurst
Branch Line to Minehead
Branch Line to Moretonhampstead
Branch Lines to Newport (IOW)
Branch Lines to Newquay
Branch Lines around North Woolwich
Branch Line to Padstow
Branch Lines around Plymouth
Branch Lines to Princes Risborough
Branch Lines to Seaton and Sidmouth
Branch Lines around Sheerness
Branch Line to Shrewsbury
Branch Line to Swanage *updated*
Branch Line to Tenterden
Branch Lines around Tiverton
Branch Lines to Torrington
Branch Lines to Tunbridge Wells
Branch Line to Upwell
Branch Lines of West London
Branch Lines of West Wiltshire
Branch Lines around Weymouth
Branch Lines around Wimborne
Branch Lines around Wisbech

NARROW GAUGE

Branch Line to Lynton
Branch Lines around Portmadoc 1923-46
Branch Lines around Porthmadog 1954-94
Branch Line to Southwold
Douglas to Port Erin
Douglas to Peel
Kent Narrow Gauge
Northern France Narrow Gauge
Romneyrail
Southern France Narrow Gauge
Sussex Narrow Gauge
Surrey Narrow Gauge
Swiss Narrow Gauge
Two-Foot Gauge Survivors
Vivarais Narrow Gauge

SOUTH COAST RAILWAYS

Ashford to Dover
Bournemouth to Weymouth
Brighton to Worthing
Eastbourne to Hastings
Hastings to Ashford
Portsmouth to Southampton
Ryde to Ventnor
Southampton to Bournemouth

SOUTHERN MAIN LINES

Basingstoke to Salisbury
Bromley South to Rochester
Crawley to Littlehampton
Dartford to Sittingbourne
East Croydon to Three Bridges
Epsom to Horsham
Exeter to Barnstaple
Exeter to Tavistock
Faversham to Dover
London Bridge to East Croydon
Orpington to Tonbridge
Tonbridge to Hastings
Salisbury to Yeovil
Sittingbourne to Ramsgate
Swanley to Ashford
Tavistock to Plymouth
Three Bridges to Brighton
Victoria to Bromley South
Victoria to East Croydon
Waterloo to Windsor
Waterloo to Woking
Woking to Portsmouth
Woking to Southampton
Yeovil to Exeter

EASTERN MAIN LINES

Barking to Southend
Ely to Kings Lynn
Ely to Norwich
Fenchurch Street to Barking
Hitchin to Peterborough
Ilford to Shenfield
Ipswich to Saxmundham
Liverpool Street to Ilford
Saxmundham to Yarmouth
Tilbury Loop

WESTERN MAIN LINES

Bristol to Taunton
Didcot to Banbury
Didcot to Swindon
Ealing to Slough
Exeter to Newton Abbot
Newton Abbot to Plymouth
Newbury to Westbury
Paddington to Ealing
Paddington to Princes Risborough
Plymouth to St. Austell
Princes Risborough to Banbury
Reading to Didcot
Slough to Newbury
St. Austell to Penzance
Swindon to Bristol
Taunton to Exeter
Westbury to Taunton

MIDLAND MAIN LINES

St. Albans to Bedford
Euston to Harrow & Wealdstone
St. Pancras to St. Albans

COUNTRY RAILWAY ROUTES

Abergavenny to Merthyr
Andover to Southampton
Bath to Evercreech Junction
Bath Green Park to Bristol
Burnham to Evercreech Junction
Cheltenham to Andover
Croydon to East Grinstead
Didcot to Winchester
East Kent Light Railway
Fareham to Salisbury
Frome to Bristol
Guildford to Redhill
Reading to Basingstoke
Reading to Guildford
Redhill to Ashford
Salisbury to Westbury
Stratford upon Avon to Cheltenham
Strood to Paddock Wood
Taunton to Barnstaple
Wenford Bridge to Fowey
Westbury to Bath
Woking to Alton
Yeovil to Dorchester

GREAT RAILWAY ERAS

Ashford from Steam to Eurostar
Clapham Junction 50 years of change
Festiniog in the Fifties
Festiniog in the Sixties
Festiniog 50 years of enterprise
Isle of Wight Lines 50 years of change
Railways to Victory 1944-46
Return to Blaenau 1970-82
SECR Centenary album
Talyllyn 50 years of change
Wareham to Swanage 50 years of change
Yeovil 50 years of change

LONDON SUBURBAN RAILWAYS

Caterham and Tattenham Corner
Charing Cross to Dartford
Clapham Jn. to Beckenham Jn.
Crystal Palace (HL) & Catford Loop
East London Line
Finsbury Park to Alexandra Palace
Holbourn Viaduct to Lewisham
Kingston and Hounslow Loops
Lewisham to Dartford
Lines around Wimbledon
Liverpool Street to Chingford
London Bridge to Addiscombe
Mitcham Junction Lines
North London Line
South London Line
West Croydon to Epsom
West London Line
Willesden Junction to Richmond
Wimbledon to Beckenham
Wimbledon to Epsom

STEAMING THROUGH

Steaming through Cornwall
Steaming through the Isle of Wight
Steaming through Kent
Steaming through West Hants

TRAMWAY CLASSICS

Aldgate & Stepney Tramways
Barnet & Finchley Tramways
Bath Tramways

Brighton's Tramways
Bristol's Tramways
Burton & Ashby Tramways
Camberwell & W.Norwood Tramways
Clapham & Streatham Tramways
Croydon's Tramways
Dover's Tramways
East Ham & West Ham Tramways
Edgware and Willesden Tramways
Eltham & Woolwich Tramways
Embankment & Waterloo Tramways
Exeter & Taunton Tramways
Fulwell - Home to Trams, Trolleys and E
Great Yarmouth Tramways
Greenwich & Dartford Tramways
Hammersmith & Hounslow Tram
Hampstead & Highgate Tramways
Hastings Tramways
Holborn & Finsbury Tramways
Ilford & Barking Tramways
Kingston & Wimbledon Tramways
Lewisham & Catford Tramways
Liverpool Tramways 1. Eastern Routes
Liverpool Tramways 2. Southern Routes
Liverpool Tramways 3. Northern Routes
Maidstone & Chatham Tramways
Margate to Ramsgate
North Kent Tramways
Norwich Tramways
Reading Tramways
Seaton & Eastbourne Tramways
Shepherds Bush & Uxbridge Tramways
Southend-on-sea Tramways
South London Line Tramways 1903
Southwark & Deptford Tramways
Stamford Hill Tramways
Twickenham & Kingston Tramway
Victoria & Lambeth Tramways
Waltham Cross & Edmonton Tramways
Walthamstow & Leyton Tramways
Wandsworth & Battersea Tramways

TROLLEYBUS CLASSICS

Croydon Trolleybuses
Derby Trolleybuses
Hastings Trolleybuses
Huddersfield Trolleybuses
Maidstone Trolleybuses
Portsmouth Trolleybuses
Reading Trolleybuses
Woolwich & Dartford Trolleybuses

WATERWAY ALBUMS

Kent and East Sussex Waterways
London to Portsmouth Waterway
West Sussex Waterways

MILITARY BOOKS

Battle over Portsmouth
Battle over Sussex 1940
Blitz over Sussex 1941-42
Bombers over Sussex 1943-45
Bognor at War
Military Defence of West Sussex
Military Signals from the South Coast
Secret Sussex Resistance
Surrey Home Guard

OTHER RAILWAY BOOKS

Index to all Middleton Press station
Industrial Railways of the South-East
South Eastern & Chatham Railways
London Chatham & Dover Railway
London Termini - Past and Proposed
War on the Line (SR 1939-45)

BIOGRAPHY

Garraway Father & Son